D1518917

Dirty Jobs

Fisher

Simon Rose

www.av2books.com

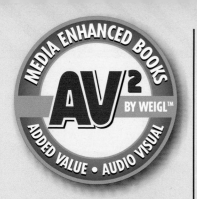

AV² provides enriched content that supplements and complements this book. Weigl's AV² books strive to create inspired learning and engage young minds in a total learning experience.

Your AV² Media Enhanced books come alive with...

Audio
Listen to sections of the book read aloud.

Key Words
Study vocabulary, and complete a matching word activity.

Go to www.av2books.com, and enter this book's unique code.

Video
Watch informative video clips.

Quizzes
Test your knowledge.

BOOK CODE

A 4 6 4 8 9 5

Embedded Weblinks
Gain additional information for research.

Slide Show
View images and captions, and prepare a presentation.

AV² by Weigl brings you media enhanced books that support active learning.

Try This!
Complete activities and hands-on experiments.

... and much, much more!

Published by AV² by Weigl
350 5th Avenue, 59th Floor
New York, NY 10118

Websites: www.av2books.com www.weigl.com

Library of Congress Cataloging-in-Publication Data
Rose, Simon, 1961-
Fisher / Simon Rose.
    pages cm. -- (Dirty jobs)
Includes index.
ISBN 978-1-4896-2986-9 (hard cover : alk. paper) -- ISBN 978-1-4896-2987-6 (soft cover : alk. paper) --
ISBN 978-1-4896-2988-3 (single user ebook) -- ISBN 978-1-4896-2989-0 (multi-user ebook)
1. Fishers--Juvenile literature. 2. Fishing boats--Juvenile literature. 3. Fisheries--Vocational guidance--Juvenile literature. I. Title.
HD8039.F65R67 2016
639.2023--dc23
                        2014038985

Printed in the United States of America in Brainerd, Minnesota
1 2 3 4 5 6 7 8 9 0 19 18 17 16 15

012015
WEP051214

Senior Editor: Aaron Carr
Designer: Mandy Christiansen

Every reasonable effort has been made to trace ownership and to obtain permission to reprint copyright material. The publishers would be pleased to have any errors or omissions brought to their attention so that they may be corrected in subsequent printings.

Weigl acknowledges Getty Images as its primary image supplier for this title.

Contents

What Is a Fisher?

A fisher is a person who catches fish or other animals from water. People who fish to earn money are known as commercial fishers. Commercial fishers and their boats need special **permits** and **licenses** to do their work. When people catch fish for fun or for sport it is called recreational fishing.

All fishers used to be called fishermen. The word fisher is now used because both men and women work in this job. Fishers need special tools and equipment. They go through training because their work can be very dangerous. Many fishers use special tools and clothing to stay safe while working.

In 2013, fishers in the United States sold nearly 1.5 billion tons (1.3 billion metric tons) of fish products to other countries.

Most fishers working far out in the ocean are men. In some countries, women work as fishers in small boats closer to shore.

There were more than **31,000** fishers working in the United States in 2012.

Commercial fishers load their catches at the wharf. The fish are then sent to the market to sell.

Where They Work

Fishers work on ships and boats. Ships are usually bigger than boats. Ships travel hundreds of miles (kilometers) **offshore**, close to the coast, or on lakes and rivers. Fishers that work in different parts of the world often catch different kinds of fish. Fishers who work far out at sea have large crews. Fishers who work in shallow water that is closer to land usually work on small boats. These boats have smaller crews.

Large fishing ships and boats that work in deep water have special equipment such as **hoists** to pull in nets that are full of fish. These ships can stay at sea for a long time. This means the fish need to be kept on ice until the ship reaches **port**. The catch might weigh tens of thousands of pounds (kilograms).

Fishing boats that work in shallow water often have a crew of only one or two people. The catch is much smaller than in large fishing ships but the boats go back to port more often to deliver the fish.

Large numbers of fish can be hauled onto the side of a boat all at once.

Fishing boats have special equipment that helps catch thousands of fish each day.

A Dirty Job

On larger ships, fishers may trim and clean fish before the ship returns to land. The fish's head and tail might be removed. The fisher might also scrape off the scales. Gutting involves cutting the fish open. The fisher has to remove parts of the fish's insides. Fish are washed to remove blood and any bacteria. Fishers sometimes need to haul very large fish onto the ship. Bites, stings, and the flick of a large fish's tail can injure fishers.

Fishers work hard and for long hours. Sometimes, they work in very rough weather and dangerous conditions. Fishers can be injured by equipment that is not working properly. They can also get caught in nets. Fishers have to deal with slippery **decks** and ice in winter.

In rough weather, fishers have to be careful about safety. If the sea is very rough, they could be washed over the side of the boat.

Fishers might be injured while at sea. This means they cannot always be looked after by a doctor. They might have to be cared for by other fishers before they can get to a doctor or a hospital.

Once the fish are caught, they are cleaned and stored until the boat reaches port.

Gutting a fish can be a very dirty job. A fisher's clothing helps protect from the fish's blood.

Commercial Fishing

Commercial fishing is very important to people who live in coastal areas. It is important that fishers do not catch too many fish. This is meant to make sure that there will always be more fish to catch.

About 6.5 billion pounds (2.9 billion kg) of edible seafood products were caught in the U.S. in 2010.

Finfish made up more than

84 percent

of these products.

52 percent

of the fish caught by U.S. fishers are caught in Alaska.

All in a Day's Work

A fisher might do a number of jobs. These depend on the fisher's job on the ship. Jobs include steering the ship and using compasses and charts. Fishers might also use **navigation** equipment such as the **Global Positioning System (GPS)**.

Some fishers are in charge of fishing operations. This mean that they tell the crew what to do. The crew might put equipment such as lines, traps, and nets in the water. This equipment also needs to be maintained and sometimes repaired while the ship is at sea. Fishers work to bring fish that are caught onto the ship. Sometimes, fish need to be measured. Some fish are put back in the sea if they are not big enough. Fish that are kept need to be sorted and stored in the ship's **hold** with salt and ice.

Fish are weighed and measured once back at the wharf. The price of the fish is based on these measurements.

People eat more than 75 percent of the world's fish production. The rest is mostly fed to animals.

In 2011, Americans ate 4.7 billion pounds (2.1 billion kg) of seafood.

More than 40 million people work in fisheries and fish farms around the world.

Chain of Command

There are many different jobs on board a fishing boat. Small boats may have a crew of five or six. Larger ships have crews of 30 or more fishers. No matter the size of the crew, each member has a job to do.

Captain

The captain is in charge of the fishing operation. He or she makes sure that the ship and equipment are working. Captains also decide what jobs everyone will do on the ship.

First Mate

The first mate is the second in command. He or she commands the ship when the captain is **off duty**. The first mate knows all about the navigation and other electronic equipment.

Deckhands

Deckhands bring large fish onto the ship. They wash and store the catch. They keep equipment and engines working properly. When the ship returns to port, deckhands tie the ship's lines to the **dock** and help unload the catch.

Boatswain

The boatswain is in charge of the deckhands. He or she works the equipment that sends out and brings in lines and nets. Boatswains take caught fish from hooks and nets.

Marine Engineer

Marine engineers make sure the ship's engine and electrical systems work properly.

Chef

The chef is in charge of preparing meals for the ship's crew.

Diver

Some ships have divers who harvest seafood such as scallops, sea urchins, and other animals that live on the sea floor.

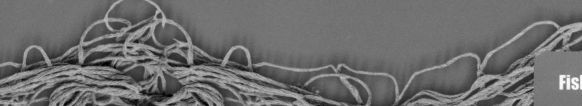

Staying Safe

There are many dangers for fishers at work. Weather conditions can change quickly on the water. Some of the equipment fishers work with, such as knives and hooks, are sharp. Fishers wear safety clothing and use safety equipment. Most fishing companies provide equipment and uniforms for their workers. Different kinds of equipment might be worn or used by fishers, depending on the type of fishing that they do.

Personal Flotation Devices (PFDs)

PFDs are also called lifejackets. Fishers wear PFDs when they are on the ship's deck. This is because they could be swept into the water. PFDs have reflective material on the outside. This helps the person be seen in the water. They have a whistle to attract attention. They inflate automatically or through a mouthpiece.

Immersion Suit

Sometimes, fishers have to abandon ship. They can die very quickly in the icy cold water. Immersion suits keep body heat in and cold water out. They also help keep fishers afloat. Immersion suits are made in bright colors. This is so that rescuers can easily see them.

Safety Glasses

Fishers might work with sharp or loose objects. Safety glasses with side shields protect the fisher's eyes. They also protect from poisonous marine animals, such as jellyfish.

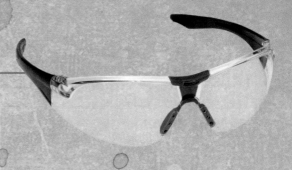

Head Protection

Fishers wear a hard hat when working under moving equipment. This also protects them from objects that can fall when unloading nets. The hard hat has a chinstrap. This keeps it from falling off when the fisher is working high up or in rough weather.

Hand Protection

Fishers use ropes that can cause burns or cut the skin. They wear gloves to protect their hands when using these ropes. Gloves also protect against the stings of some fish. Fishers wear gloves when taking fish off hooks. They also wear gloves when using knives to clean fish or chop **bait**.

Tools of the Trade

Fishers have many tools that they use in their work. Many different types of nets are used to catch fish. Hoists are used by fishers to pull nets full of fish up from the water. Fishers also use sharp hooks to haul some of the larger fish onto the deck of the ship. Today, fishers use electronic equipment, such as satellite systems that give information about where the vessel is, the weather, and wave patterns.

Nets

The net used depends on the type of fish being caught. It also depends on location and weather. Most nets are long, narrow, and flat. They have floats on top and weights on the bottom. These keep part of the net on the surface of the water and part of it on the ocean floor. This keeps the net open so the fish will go into it.

Hooks

The hook used depends on the type of fish that is being caught. Hooks are often baited with smaller fish or insects to attract the fish. A gaff is a hooked pole. It is used for pulling large and heavy fish onto the boat.

Lines

A fishing line is a long piece of cord usually made from artificial materials, such as nylon. Long lines have shorter lines called snoods attached to them. There are anchors at each end of the line. Floats keep the line near the surface. For **trawling**, baited hooks on lines are towed behind a ship or boat.

Radar and Sonar

Fishers use electronic equipment called radar and sonar to find fish. Radar finds objects moving above the surface of the water. They show up as blips on a ship's radar screen. Sonar is used to find underwater objects, such as large schools of fish.

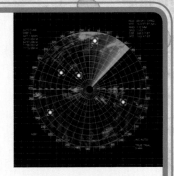

Then

In the past, fishers might not have always been able to find enough fish, even in well-known fishing areas. Sometimes, ships had to return to port with a very small catch. Fishing ships and boats were dangerous places to work. Fishers did not have safety clothing. This created more accidents.

Now

Today, fishing ships and boats use electronic equipment for navigation. Large ships can also stay at sea longer to catch more fish. They use technology, such as sonar equipment, that can work out how many fish are in a certain area. Fishing is still dangerous, but fishers are better protected today.

The Fisher's Role

There will be fewer fishing jobs in the coming years. However, fishers are very important to the U.S. economy. In Alaska, 20 percent of all jobs are in the seafood industry. Fishing is also very important in other states. Many fishers are seasonal workers. They do not do the job all year round. In Alaska, the salmon season is in the summer. The number of fishers more than doubles at this time.

Salmon are quite small fish, but they are caught in large numbers in nets.

Overfishing is lowering the numbers of some types of fish. Turtles and other ocean animals are also sometimes caught in fishing nets. The food supply of marine animals can be hurt by lower fish numbers. Governments make new laws to protect fish, but there are still problems.

The Seafood Industry

The seafood industry grew in the U.S. as each coastal area was settled. Early coastal communities caught and sold fish and other ocean animals. Fishing became part of their way of life. Today, many small communities still rely on fishing. Most of the local jobs are in fishing or seafood processing.

Seafood brings about **$3 billion** to the people and businesses of Alaska each year.

There are more than **one million** jobs in the U.S. seafood industry.

About **one** of every **three** fish caught are taken from the northwestern Pacific Ocean.

More than **90 percent** of all fishers work on small ships and boats.

Becoming a Fisher

To be a fisher, people need the right skills and attitude. The job has long hours and is hard work. Fishers also spend a great deal of time away from home. Sometimes, this is far out at sea for many weeks or months. It is important to be in good physical shape to be a fisher. Working conditions may also be uncomfortable. If the sea is very rough, fishers must be careful when moving around on the deck. Work is also often seasonal. This means the job is only for part of the year.

Salaries

Salaries for workers in the fishing industry vary in different areas. Salaries are usually higher in the summer and fall. They are lowest in the winter. The salaries of fishers depend on their job on the ship and if they are one of the ship's owners. The money earned also depends on the size of the ship and the value of the catch. U.S. fishers earn an average yearly salary of $33,430 and the average hourly rate is $11.34. The captain of a ship or boat earns more than the workers.

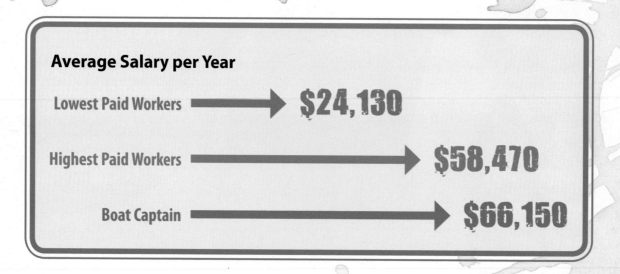

Average Salary per Year

Lowest Paid Workers → **$24,130**

Highest Paid Workers → **$58,470**

Boat Captain → **$66,150**

Halibut are caught off the coast of Alaska. They are gutted on board the ship.

Is This Career For You?

Careers in the fishing industry are not for everyone. Even if you have some or all of the skills needed, you might be uncomfortable working on ships and boats. If you feel this way during your early training at sea, the feeling is unlikely to go away. You may need to think about a different career. Most fishers are either **self-employed** or they work in small companies.

✓ Training

Commercial fishers usually train on the job. Most start as deckhands. They learn the work from other crew members. An experienced fisher can rise to become a boatswain, first mate, or captain.

✓ Education

No formal education is required to be a fisher. Sometimes, there are programs at high schools in coastal areas. Students learn how to operate and navigate ships and boats. They also learn how to handle fishing equipment. Operators of large ships need to complete training approved by the U.S. Coast Guard.

✓ Application

Fishers often find work through family or friends. Some people visit the docks and ask about available jobs. Companies that operate large ships often have a special department, known as a human resource department, that employs people for their ships.

Career Connections Activity

Plan your fishing career with this activity. Follow the instructions in the steps below to complete the process of becoming a fisher.

1. If you live in a coastal area, speak to local fishers. They can answer your questions and give you an inside look into the profession.

2. Visit a job fair or a college career center to find out more information about working in the fishing industry.

4. Call or write to a fishing company. Say that you are interested in a fishing job and ask for advice on how to apply.

3. Work on your resumé. A good resumé that shows your strongest skills can go a long way toward attracting the attention of potential employers.

1. Decide if you have the personality and attitude for being a fisher. You might need to be at sea for many hours, maybe even overnight, or many days.

2. Consider the skills you will need to have. Being comfortable at sea will be a big help. If you are able to navigate and steer a boat, this will also help.

3. Speak to someone who is already doing the job. It might be a deckhand, or it might be a ship's captain.

4. Tell the people you meet that you would like a job. When you go to the interview, be confident about your skills and the reasons why you want a job as a fisher.

Quiz

1. What is a gaff?

2. Who is the second in command on a fishing vessel after the captain?

3. What is seasonal work?

4. How many commercial fishers were working in the United States in 2012?

5. What are Personal Flotation Devices (PFDs) also called?

6. How many U.S. jobs does the seafood industry support?

7. What is it called when people catch fish for pleasure or for sport?

8. What is sonar used for?

9. In which state was 52 percent of the total U.S. fish catch in 2010?

10. What was the average salary per year of a U.S. fisher in 2012?

Answers: 1. A hooked pole used for landing large and heavy fish **2.** The first mate **3.** Work that is only for part of the year **4.** More than 31,000 **5.** Lifejackets **6.** More than one million **7.** Recreational fishing **8.** To locate objects underwater **9.** Alaska **10.** $33,430

Key Words

bait: food used to attract fish or other animals

decks: the floors of a ship or boat

dock: a structure on the shore to which boats may be tied up

Global Positioning system (GPS): a system used to find where something is located

hoists: kinds of machinery that lift heavy objects

hold: the lower cargo deck of a ship or boat

licenses: documents that are proof that a permission has been given

navigation: the process of directing the course of a ship

off duty: taking a break from one's work

offshore: located at a distance away from the shore

permits: documents that give permission to do something, such as fishing in a certain place

port: a harbor where ships load or unload

self-employed: working for oneself rather than for an employer.

trawling: towing a long fishing line behind a boat with baited hooks for catching fish

Index

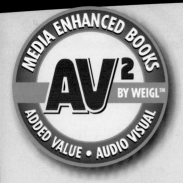

Log on to www.av2books.com

AV[2] by Weigl brings you media enhanced books that support active learning. Go to www.av2books.com, and enter the special code found on page 2 of this book. You will gain access to enriched and enhanced content that supplements and complements this book. Content includes video, audio, weblinks, quizzes, a slide show, and activities.

AV[2] Online Navigation

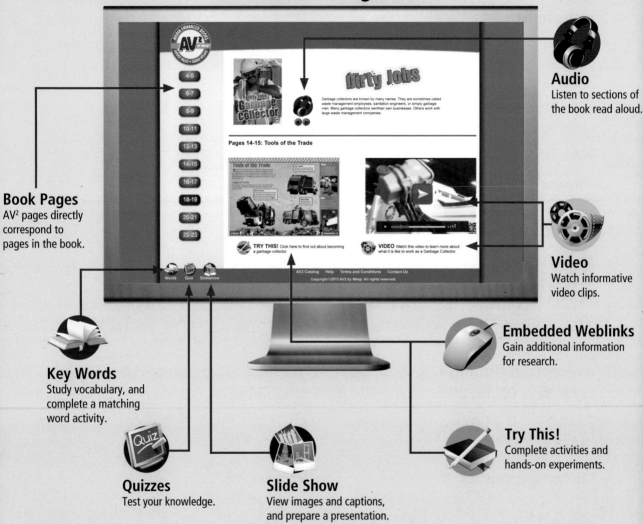

Book Pages
AV[2] pages directly correspond to pages in the book.

Audio
Listen to sections of the book read aloud.

Video
Watch informative video clips.

Key Words
Study vocabulary, and complete a matching word activity.

Embedded Weblinks
Gain additional information for research.

Quizzes
Test your knowledge.

Slide Show
View images and captions, and prepare a presentation.

Try This!
Complete activities and hands-on experiments.

AV[2] was built to bridge the gap between print and digital. We encourage you to tell us what you like and what you want to see in the future.

Sign up to be an AV[2] Ambassador at www.av2books.com/ambassador.